October

October

Poems

Eva Eliav

© 2026 Eva Eliav. All rights reserved.
This material may not be reproduced in any form, published,
reprinted, recorded, performed, broadcast,
rewritten or redistributed without
the explicit permission of Eva Eliav.
All such actions are strictly prohibited by law.

Cover design by Shay Culligan
Cover image by K8 on Unsplash

ISBN: 979-8-90146-706-0

Kelsay Books
502 South 1040 East, A-119
American Fork, Utah 84003
Kelsaybooks.com

Acknowledgments

Many thanks to the publications in which poems from *October* have appeared:

MacQueen's Quinterly

Minyan Magazine

One Art

Panoplyzine

Thimble

Contents

2023

our days	15
angel	18
rainbow	20
pompeii	21
when evil came	22
growth	23
stream	24
cocoons	25
mountain	26
fury rumbles	27
mother nature	29
first rain	30
rain	31
leaks	32
signal	33

2024

sacrifice	37
hybrid morning	38
last night	39
lost	40
ungathered	41
four in the morning	42
we're fine	44
october sixth	45
october seventh	46
october eighth	47

invasion	48
hell opened	49
afterwards	50
I pass a woman	51
we grow old	52
Yom Kippur	53
my throat hurts	54
dream	55
last dance	56
shelter	57

2023

our days

1.
my eyes rest on the photos
of the dead

faces alight with confidence
with laughter

moments pass

I have errands
obligations

a dark current surges
against my will

2.
a sign of age I think
this wondering

this tender
and ferocious
backward glance

sunlight tears its way
through smooth gray sky

lays its fingers
warm
against my skin

3.
I chase the days
like children playing tag

I am no match for them
so quick and light

they leave me
in the dust

4.
fear an animal
that lives in me

wild
yet domestic

hungry
for morsels
of sunlight

5.
shadows of leaves
converse with one another

urgent
quick

a language
the deaf speak

a silent commotion

6.
in this space
I shift
to another dimension

hopes I have lost
gallop home

angel

I met an angel

who looked
nothing
like an angel

an old fat man
who smoked too much

breathed heavily

spent his days
sitting on a bench

idly
intersecting
with my life

today
he greeted me

he offered words

light carved
from his throat

don't be afraid
he said

it will be all right

rainbow

an accident
of birth

rain and sun
colliding
before we vanish

pompeii

preserved
in their ordeal
the remnants speak

eggs in a pot
waiting to be served

a little dog eager
to flee outside

forever thwarted
by a storm of ash

when evil came

when evil came
it was a quiet morning

no one imagined
what the hours
would bring

evil gorged
on a sumptuous feast
of pain

lapped blood
and smacked its lips

we were left
with burning

with the ashes

growth

something's growing
on my hand

it looks like
flower petals

or tentacles
of a tiny octopus

a seed fell
in the garden
of my flesh

my aging skin
desiccated
dry

welcomes
a spear of growth

stream

yarn flows
through my fingers

over them
between them

a rainbow stream
of grace

cocoons

we weave cocoons
to shelter
and contain us

risky to poke a finger

wriggle toes

any moment
cruelty
may erupt

tear our courage
into shreds
of flesh and blood

mountain

scaling
a jagged mountain

the peak has vanished
and the air grows thin

our map fell
like a stone

we left behind cinders
that were children

a storm is raging

fury rumbles

fury rumbles

distant
as a storm cloud

how can I lure it back
into my heart

resurrect the ashes

become the fire

prayers

where is the living god
in all of this

strong hands
atrophied
or hidden

shelter was never
provided

though it was promised

even an illusion
served us well

we pushed ourselves
sunward
between betrayals

mother nature

some instinct
drives it all

like newborn fawns
delectable to lions

our children are dismembered
and devoured

though they are luminous
though they are brave

nature fails us
in a million ways

first rain

so much depends
on faith

and on the weather

clouds move heavily
scattering seeds
at dawn

artillery more melodious
than love songs

rain

it's turning out to be
one of those winters

skies burdened with rain
aching with rain

pigeons
hugging themselves
against the wall

I wake reluctantly

seeking safety
from a hostile dawn

endless cups of tea
are never hot enough
or sweet enough

leaks

the ceiling leaks

beneath it
papers curl

words become diluted
into stains

oddly shaped
pellucid

wondrous
as sea glass

signal

night comes
yet the day is
incomplete

I wander restlessly

wait for a signal
from the universe

as a child sits
on a slide

pensive and still
listening

holding fast

2024

sacrifice

purged of hope
we walked out to the fields

long-time lovers
fingers intertwined

a sacrifice
willing
and unwilling

battalions of angels
cleared our way

their pity wiped our tears

hybrid morning

this hybrid morning

two birds preen
on the wall

one white
one black

how tenderly
they care for one another

nearby
two missiles fall

shrapnel tears flesh

last night

last night
rockets burst overhead

walls shuddered

neighbours crouched
in the stairwell
comforting one another

a blur of heartbeats

hummingbirds sucking sweetness
from the moment

lost

disturbing dreams

I flee
between one home
and another

phone held
tight as hope

safety unreachable
at either number

ungathered

faith liquefies

slides like rain
through particles of sand

slides through hearts

helpless to gather it

four in the morning

at four in the morning
I make a bold decision

I won't collect my mail
won't open it
won't file it

briefly I wonder
if I should read and filter
before the bin gobbles it whole
like a dog's supper

decide against wondering

I'll free myself
from choices
that don't matter

what matters is
this war
this war
this war

what matters is
that evil's rampaging

pulling terrible faces
screeching
grinning

proudly filming itself
for posterity

good people
fold themselves so small
they take no room at all

we're fine

we're fine we say

though all of us could easily qualify
to enter the emotional paralympics

win gold
silver and bronze
a clean sweep

october sixth

october sixth

the weather's perfect
warm with a cool breeze

we circulate

wish family and friends
a better year

bring jars of hope
a sweet and bitter honey

october seventh

october seventh

a time for grief
emptiness
surrender

respecting what is owed
fullness of weeping

october eighth

October eighth

in darkness
a splash of fire

the order of nature
tipped over

in the end
words

invasion

I have to wonder
how they managed to round up
so many killers

did they put up posters
advertise

glorious freedom offered
to monsters uncomfortably
squeezed
behind human faces

hell opened

before hell opened
and its inhabitants
scurried out

I was sure the pit
was fantasy
created to frighten children
into virtue

the monsters that occasionally
popped up
were hideous exceptions
to the rule

not harbingers
of an immense army

an anthill
swarming with darkness

afterwards

afterwards

the ribcage closes
tightly
around its lungs

the heart lifts its drawbridge shut

the mantras of innocence
fall silent

I pass a woman

I pass a woman
sitting on a bench

she wipes her nose
a furtive gesture

she is weeping

we grow old

we grow old within
our walls
of fragile bone

lucky to grow old

Yom Kippur

Yom Kippur

pale blue souls
hung out

billowing

earth relishes its banquet
of flesh and blood

licks its lips

doesn't ask forgiveness

my throat hurts

my throat hurts

perhaps a scream
withheld
a knotted grief

I've listened to
my morning meditation

a man pushes his walker
past my table

moving forward
past all he has endured

dream

small animals
knowing there is no hope
grow very still

in silence
men dig graves

lick traces of life's flavour
from their lips

women wait and watch
whispering words of comfort
to their children

babes in arms are somber
as old souls

all is foreseen
all must be endured

I wake screaming

last dance

our children danced

our children danced
and bled

the vessels of their bodies
broke and spilled

the night-warm earth
grew salty
with their blood

perhaps in the larger scheme
all works for good

here chaos rules

shelter

within the dunes

dryness floods
with meaning

hearts drink deep

butterflies
shelter
among the cacti

thorns miraculously
soften

the air quivers

About the Author

Eva Eliav received her B.A. in English Language and Literature from The University of Toronto. She is the author of two poetry chapbooks: *Eve* (Red Bird Chapbooks, 2019) and *One Summer Day* (Kelsay Books, 2021). A new chapbook is forthcoming from Red Bird.

Her poetry and flash fiction have appeared in numerous literary journals, including *Room, Emrys Journal, JewishFiction.net, Ilanot Review, Flashquake, The Apple Valley Review, Horizon Review, Variant Lit, Luna Station Quarterly, Fairy Tale Magazine, Stand, Constellations, Minyan Magazine, Fictive Dream, Gyroscope Review, MacQueen's Quinterly, Rogue Agent, Dust, Thimble, The Lake Magazine, One Art, Panoplyzine,* and *The Ginosko Review.*

You can find a selection of her poetry, fiction, and art at:
www.evaeliav.com

www.ingramcontent.com/pod-product-compliance
Lightning Source LLC
Chambersburg PA
CBHW031422160426
43196CB00008B/1018